COCKTAIL
BOTANICA

60+ drinks inspired by nature

COCKTAIL BOTANICA

ELOUISE ANDERS

ILLUSTRATIONS ᴮʏ ANNABELLE LAMBIE

Smith Street Books

Contents

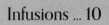

Introduction

Refreshing, natural and distinct, the use of botanical ingredients when creating cocktails has taken centre stage in the drinks world. The lurid blues, glacé cherries and paper umbrellas, while not gone, have certainly fallen a little down the list of essential ingredients.

If you search the menus of the world's best cocktail bars, you'll find cocoa, jasmine, sage, tomato - a wealth of natural ingredients mixed with top spirits to make magic in a glass,

The pairing of natural flavours with spirits is nothing new – the very process of creating many of the world's best spirits, including one of the most popular, gin, is to include plants to create new and exciting flavours. Gin's origins can be traced as far back as the 11th century, when Italian monks distilled spirits with juniper berries, in an attempt to mask the unpleasant taste of the spirit. Back then it was a tonic used for medicinal purposes, but by the 17th century the rise of the juniper-infused drink, known by the Dutch as *jenever*, eventually shortened to gin, became a mainstay in England. Now, a few hundred years later, the gin we see on the shelves has been made with a vast array of botanical ingredients, an explosion of flavour experimentation.

While the concept may seem daunting, in reality the process of infusing your own spirits to use in your cocktails is pretty easy and the combinations you can produce are limitless. The process of taking the time – sometimes a few days and sometimes just a few minutes – to create something that is specific to your tastes is easy to do at home and requires next to no set-up.

Adding something fresh and floral to a drink on a hot day can transport you to the great outdoors where you can almost smell the roses. Something a bit more earthy, like fresh ginger or rosemary, can warm your body and your mind. The fruit-based cocktail will never go out of fashion, and a good punch is a lifesaver when you have a crowd to entertain. So, step inside the glorious world of the botanical cocktail, where every ingredient can be hand-picked to suit no-one, but you.

On equipment

Getting started at home is so easy, there are just a few basic tips to remember:

- Jars or containers used for infusing should be washed with hot, soapy water and dried before use.

- Since most of the bottles spirits come in have a small bottle opening, you'll need to infuse in a different container - canning or mason jars work well and come with a handy lid.

- Choose the correct size jar or container for the amount you are planning to make - these infusion recipes can be easily scaled up or down to suit your needs.

- Aim to fill the jars almost completely, so that any fresh ingredients are fully submerged.

- When you are happy with your infusion, strain the liquid through a fine sieve into a clean jug to remove the solids. You can then strain a second time through a muslin-lined cloth to remove any small bits and sediment.

- Once you've made your infusion, you can store it back in the bottle it came in, just remember to label it to avoid any mix-ups and store in a cool, dark place for the longest shelf life. Infused spirits can be stored for up to a year.

On infusing

The beauty of infusing at home is that it's all about your personal preference - what spirit, what flavours, and the strength of the infusion are all free for you to tweak to your own tastes. The infusion recipes here are just a guide - there's no limit to what amazing (and sometimes wacky) flavours you can come up with, although it can be a lesson to start small - garlic vodka is good in a Bloody Mary but might not be so palatable in a Paloma! The same can be said about the base spirits or wines you use - when starting out, keep the top shelf for another use.

On gathering and preparing

While the thought of wandering through the fields as you forage for the freshest and brightest ingredients for your heavenly concoctions sounds ideal, foraging for botanicals should always be done with equal parts enthusiasm and caution – it is essential that any ingredients picked from the wild are properly identified to ensure they are edible. As the saying goes: if in doubt, leave it out.

Also:

- Gourmet food stores or online retailers often sell harder to find ingredients, including dried and fresh, edible flower varieties.

- Prepare herbs as you would for cooking, and wash the outer rinds and skin of anything that you will be using to infuse. Flowers should be lightly brushed to remove any dirt and any inedible parts removed before using (see note on identification above).

- Some infused syrups are best when left to infuse overnight, so read the recipes in full before breaking out the drinks trolley.

- Always take extreme caution when heating any alcohol, as it is highly flammable.

On garnishing

When it comes to botanical cocktails, the bigger the better when it comes to garnishes! Whole flowers, sticks of vegetables – you can really use them to make an impression. Try some smaller edible flowers, micro herbs or fruit leaves frozen into ice cubes to add a beautiful botanical flourish to your cocktails.

INFUSIONS

A good way to dip your toe into the wonderful world of infusions is to start with what you know, and the mix of strawberry and basil has been well established as a dynamic duo. In order for the strawberry to sing, it goes in first, before the stronger, pungent basil is added.

Strawberry & Basil Vodka

250 g (9 oz) strawberries

750 ml (3 cups) vodka

1 small bunch basil

Wash, hull and quarter the strawberries, then place them into a clean 1 litre (4 cup) capacity jar or container with a lid (see page 8). Pour in the vodka, ensuring the fruit is fully covered. Cover with the lid then shake gently.

Place the jar in a cool, dark place for 2–3 days, gently shaking it each day.

Wash the basil and then add it to the jar. Close the lid and shake gently, then leave for a further 2–3 days. Taste the infusion after 2 days to check if you are happy with the flavour, leaving for another day if you want a stronger flavour.

Pass the vodka through a muslin-lined strainer into a jug, discarding the solids. Transfer to a clean bottle or jar, seal and use as desired.

MAKES 750 ML (3 CUPS)

There's no need to be restricted to the pedestrian (but delicious) flavours of lemon and orange, you can use any citrus – think lime, grapefruit, mandarin, yuzu – all would work well here. The white pith can be very bitter, so it's worth taking the time to remove it.

Citrus Vodka

2 lemons

1 orange or blood orange

750 ml (3 cups) vodka

Wash the lemons and orange, then use a vegetable peeler to peel the zest from the fruit, leaving behind as much of the white pith as you can manage. Keep the rest of the fruit for another use. Place the zest into a clean 1 litre (4 cup) capacity jar or container with a lid (see page 8). Pour in the vodka, ensuring the zest is fully covered. Cover with the lid then shake gently.

Place the jar in a cool, dark place for 5–7 days, gently shaking it each day.

Taste the infusion after 5 days to check if you are happy with the flavour, leaving for longer if you want a stronger flavour.

Pass the vodka through a strainer into a jug, discarding the zest. Transfer to a clean bottle or jar, seal and use as desired.

MAKES 750 ML (3 CUPS)

While this may sound a little strange, garlic can impart a wonderful savoury flavour to your drinks. Use it in a Herby bloody Mary (page 76), conjure up your own garlic Dirty martini, or add it to a vodka pasta sauce. Once you have it, you'll find plenty of ways to use it.

Garlic Vodka

1 bulb of garlic

1 long red chilli (optional)

750 ml (3 cups) vodka

Separate the garlic cloves and peel them, then use a knife to cut off the small woody stem. Wash and halve the chilli, if using. Place the cloves and chilli into a clean 1 litre (4 cup) capacity jar or container with a lid (see page 8). Pour in the vodka, cover with the lid and shake gently.

After 30 minutes, taste the infusion to check the strength of the garlic and chilli, leaving for a further 30 minutes (maximum 1–2 hours) if needed until it has reached your desired level of flavour.

Pass the vodka through a muslin-lined strainer into a jug, discarding the solids. Transfer to a clean bottle or jar, seal and use as desired.

MAKES 750 ML (3 CUPS)

Chocolate-flavoured vodka can be bought from liquor stores, but it often comes with a hefty amount of added sugar, which can make your mixed drinks a bit too sickly sweet. Make your own instead to enjoy a cleaner version, and you could even add a split vanilla bean.

Chocolate Vodka

3 tablespoons cacao nibs

40 g (1½ oz) dark chocolate

750 ml (3 cups) vodka

Place the cacao nibs into a mortar and use a pestle to roughly crush. Chop the chocolate into small pieces. Place the cacao nibs and chocolate into a clean 1 litre (4 cup) capacity jar or container with a lid (see page 8). Add the vodka, cover with the lid then shake gently to combine.

Place the jar in a cool, dark place. Taste the infusion after 2 days to check if you are happy with the flavour, leaving for longer if you want a stronger flavour.

Pass the vodka through a muslin-lined strainer into a jug, discarding the solids. Transfer to a clean bottle or jar, seal and use as desired.

MAKES 750 ML (3 CUPS)

Pears have a long alcohol-tinged history. Aside from perry, a cider-like beverage made from the fruit, they've also long been distilled to make fruit brandy. There are over 3,000 varieties of this ancient fruit, so you'll surely be able to find one that suits your own particular taste.

Vanilla & Pear Gin

3–4 small pears

750 ml (3 cups) gin

1 vanilla bean, split lengthways

Wash the pears, removing the stalks, then cut each into quarters and remove the core. Place the pears into a clean 1 litre (4 cup) capacity jar or container with a lid (see page 8). Pour in the gin, ensuring the fruit is fully covered. Cover with the lid then shake gently.

Place the jar in a cool, dark place, for 4 days, gently shaking it each day. On the fourth day, add the vanilla bean to the jar, cover the jar again and shake. Return to the cool, dark place for 3–4 more days, tasting daily until you are happy with the flavour.

Pass the gin through a muslin-lined strainer into a jug, discarding the solids. Transfer to a clean bottle or jar, seal and use as desired.

MAKES 750 ML (3 CUPS)

Butterfly pea flowers are native to Asia, and their vibrant peacock-blue hue has caused them to be used as a natural dye for food, drink and textiles. The buds are said to be rich in antioxidants, with butterfly pea flower tea a staple in health food stores. The addition of an acid to liquid containing the flowers turns the bright blue to a rich purple - pure magic!

Blue Floral Gin

4–6 fresh lavender sprigs

1 tablespoon dried edible butterfly pea flowers

750 ml (3 cups) gin

Pick the lavender flowers from the sprigs and place them into a clean jar or container with a lid. Add the butterfly pea flowers and the gin then stir well to combine, then cover with the lid.

Leave to infuse for 2–3 hours then taste – the flavours will get stronger the longer you leave them to infuse.

Pass the gin through a muslin-lined strainer into a jug, discarding the solids. Transfer to a clean bottle or jar, seal and use as desired.

MAKES 750 ML (3 CUPS)

Cucumber and mint are both characterised by their cool, refreshing flavours, which in turn make wonderful cool, refreshing cocktails. While infusing, the gin will take on a pale green colour. This one needs only a splash of tonic water and some ice to make it a perfect ten.

Cucumber & Mint Gin

1 long cucumber

1 small bunch mint

750 ml (3 cups) gin

Peel, deseed and slice the cucumber, then place it and the mint into a clean 1 litre (4 cup) capacity jar or container with a lid (see page 8). Pour in the gin, ensuring the cucumber and mint are fully covered. Cover with the lid then shake gently.

Place the jar in a cool, dark place for 1–2 days, gently shaking each day. Taste the infusion after 2 days to check if you are happy with the flavour, leaving for longer if you want a stronger flavour.

Pass the gin through a muslin-lined strainer into a jug, discarding the solids. Transfer to a clean bottle or jar, seal and use as desired.

MAKES 750 ML (3 CUPS)

These pretty little flowers can be found growing wild in many locations and are easy to pick and harvest if you are lucky enough to live in one of those places. Alas, if not, then the widely available buds are easy to use and will give you the same lovely, calming flavour.

Chamomile Gin

½ cup dried edible chamomile flowers

750 ml (3 cups) gin

Place the flowers and gin into a clean 1 litre (4 cup) capacity jar or container with a lid (see page 8). Cover with the lid and shake gently.

Taste the infusion after 1–2 days to check if you are happy with the flavour, leaving for longer if you want a stronger flavour.

Pass the gin through a muslin-lined strainer into a jug, discarding the solids. Transfer to a clean bottle or jar, seal and use as desired.

MAKES 750 ML (3 CUPS)

These rum-soaked cherries and the ruby liquid they leave behind might not last long in your fridge! We've upgraded from moonshine - the term for high percentage alcohol that was illegally made under the moonlight - to rum, but you could just as easily use vodka.

Cherry Rum & Moonshine Cherries

300 g (10½ oz) fresh cherries

750 ml (3 cups) white rum

115 g (½ cup) caster (superfine) sugar

Sterilise a 1 litre (4 cup) capacity heatproof jar with a lid. Wash the cherries well, removing any stems, then pit them and place them into the jar.

Place 250 ml (1 cup) of the rum and the sugar into a small saucepan, then very carefully heat over a low flame (see page 9), stirring until the sugar dissolves, then remove from the heat and leave to cool slightly. Pour the sugar–rum mixture and remaining rum over the cherries, close with the lid then gently swirl to combine.

Store in a cool, dark place for 1 week, then transfer to the fridge for a further week. The cherries and rum will keep in the fridge for up to 6 months.

MAKES 750 ML (3 CUPS)

The tropical pineapple naturally lends itself to a pairing with rum, so often the main spirit in tropical tiki concoctions. White rum, aged briefly and usually in steel vats, and gold rum, aged for longer in oak barrels, both work well here, taking on the fruity pineapple flavour.

Pineapple Rum

1 pineapple

750 ml (3 cups) white or gold rum

Peel the pineapple and cut into chunks, then place them into a clean 1 litre (4 cup) capacity jar or container with a lid (see page 8). Pour in the rum, covering the pineapple completely. Cover with the lid then shake gently.

Store in a cool, dark place, gently shaking and tasting every 1–2 days, for up to 1 week, until you are happy with the flavour.

Pass the rum through a muslin-lined strainer into a jug, discarding the solids. Transfer to a clean bottle or jar, seal and use as desired.

MAKES 750 ML (3 CUPS)

The habanero chilli comes in at about a '7' on the scale of '1' to 'my mouth is literally on fire', so use with extreme caution, removing the seeds and inner membranes if you are heat-shy. Use this infusion when your usual tequila-based cocktails are in need of a little fire.

Habanero & Lime Tequila

5 limes

750 ml (3 cups) tequila blanco

1 habanero chilli

Wash the limes, then use a vegetable peeler to peel the zest from the fruit, leaving behind as much of the white pith as you can manage. Place the zest into a clean 1 litre (4 cup) capacity jar or container with a lid (see page 8). Pour in the tequila, then cover with the lid and shake gently.

Place the jar in a cool, dark place for 3–4 days, gently shaking it each day.

Wash the habanero then thinly slice, taking care to protect your hands and eyes. Add the habanero to the jar, close tightly and give the jar a shake. After 30 minutes, taste the infusion to check the strength of the chilli – leave for a further 30 minutes (maximum 1–2 hours) until it has reached your desired level of spiciness.

Pass the tequila through a muslin-lined strainer into a jug, discarding the solids. Transfer to a clean bottle or jar, seal and use as desired.

MAKES 750 ML (3 CUPS)

Aromatic ginger and lemongrass, staples in South-East Asian cuisine, pair well and hold their bold flavours when used to infuse spirits. While tequila comes from Latin America, this marriage of flavours works perfectly and is versatile enough for a range of cocktails.

Lemongrass & Ginger Tequila

2 large pieces ginger

3 lemongrass stalks

750 ml (3 cups) tequila blanco

Peel the ginger and slice thinly. Slice the roots off the lemongrass stalks and peel the outer leaves, then slice the white piece of the stalk and discard the rest. Place the ginger, lemongrass and tequila into a clean 1 litre (4 cup) capacity jar or container with a lid (see page 8). Cover with the lid and shake gently.

Place the jar in a cool, dark place for 5–7 days, gently shaking and tasting it each day until you are happy with the flavours.

Pass the tequila through a muslin-lined strainer into a jug, discarding the solids. Transfer to a clean bottle or jar, seal and use as desired.

MAKES 750 ML (3 CUPS)

The old Irish word for whiskey is *uisce beatha*, which literally translates as 'water of life' – giving some indication as to how far it has permated cultures over hundreds of years. Perfect for the colder months, this infusion will put a spiced-apple fire in your belly.

Cinnamon & Apple Whiskey

2 red apples

750 ml (3 cups) whiskey

5 cinnamon sticks

Wash the apples, removing the stalks, then cut each into quarters, remove the core then thinly slice each quarter. Place the apples into a clean 1 litre (4 cup) capacity jar or container with a lid (see page 8). Pour in the whiskey, ensuring the apples are fully covered. Cover with the lid then gently shake.

Place the jar in a cool, dark place. After 3–4 days, add the cinnamon sticks, close the jar and gently shake. Return to the dark place for a further 3–4 days, tasting daily until you are happy with the flavour.

Pass the whiskey through a muslin-lined strainer into a jug, discarding the solids. Transfer to a clean bottle or jar, seal and use as desired.

MAKES 750 ML (3 CUPS)

Wine already has its own lovely flavour, but let's live a little. Avoid using anything too cheap here, as unpleasant wine will just produce an infused unpleasant wine. This recipe is a great way to freshen up a bottle that has been hanging around in the fridge for a bit too long.

Lemon Rose

small handful lemon balm leaves

1 lemon

1 bottle rose wine

Wash the lemon balm and outer skin of the lemon. Slice the lemon, then place the slices, along with the lemon balm, into a clean carafe or 1 litre (4 cup) capacity jar with a lid. Pour over the wine, then cover and leave to infuse for 1–2 days in the fridge, gently stirring every once in a while.

Strain before serving. Serve chilled.

SERVES 5

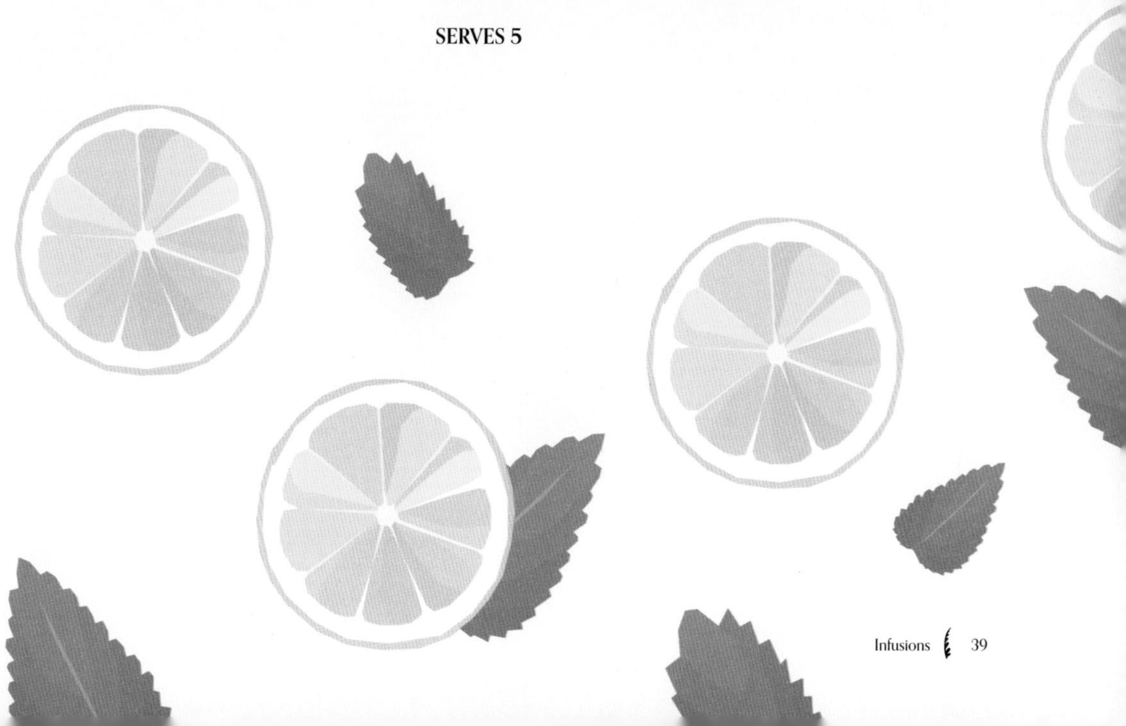

The delicate flavour of raspberry and mint brighten up a bottle of white and add a garden tea party vibe to any gathering. The raspberries can, of course, be eaten, and rose makes a lovely substitute for white wine, if desired. Sun hats and finger sandwiches go well with this infusion.

Raspberry & Mint Wine

small handful mint

125 g (1 cup) raspberries

1 bottle white wine

Wash the mint and raspberries well, then place into a clean carafe or 1 litre (4 cup) capacity jar with a lid.

Pour over the wine, then cover and leave to infuse for 1–2 days in the fridge.

Strain before serving. Serve chilled.

SERVES 5

FLORAL

The wild hibiscus has of late become a cocktail ingredient du jour - the flowers are blood-red and come preserved in a ruby-hued syrup which can also be used. Take the time to watch the bud unfurl in the bubbling wine, adding a romantic, dreamy appearance to this spritz.

Wild Hibiscus Fizz

1 hibiscus flower in syrup, plus 15 ml (½ fl oz) of the syrup

ice cubes

30 ml (1 fl oz) vodka

20 ml (¾ fl oz) lemon juice

chilled Prosecco, to top

Use a long-handled spoon to gently place the hibiscus flower on the bottom of a champagne flute.

Fill a cocktail shaker with ice and add the hibiscus syrup, vodka and lemon juice. Shake well for 15 seconds until well combined then strain into the champagne flute. Top with chilled Prosecco.

SERVES 1

Every year the heady scent of fresh marigolds is used to guide the spirits of the dead from their world, back to their homes and living loved ones on Día de los Muertos, the Day of the Dead. Believe what you will, this festive marigold-infused tipple will certainly revive you.

Marigold Margarita

55 g (¼ cup) caster (superfine) sugar

1 tablespoon dried edible marigold petals, plus 1 teaspoon extra to garnish

1 teaspoon salt

lime wedge

ice cubes

45 ml (1½ fl oz) tequila

30 ml (1 fl oz) Cointreau

30 ml (1 fl oz) lime juice

1 fresh marigold, to garnish (optional)

Make a marigold syrup by combining the sugar, dried marigold petals and 60 ml (¼ cup) water in a small saucepan. Bring to the boil and stir until the sugar dissolves. Remove from the heat and leave to infuse for 30 minutes, then strain into a small bowl, discarding the solids.

Place the salt and remaining dried marigold petals on a small plate and mix to combine. Run a lime wedge around the rim of a chilled margarita glass, then dip the rim in the marigold salt. Set aside.

Fill a cocktail shaker with ice and add the tequila, Cointreau, lime juice and 25 ml (¾ fl oz) of the marigold syrup. Shake well for 30 seconds then strain into the prepared glass. Garnish with a fresh marigold, if using.

The remaining marigold syrup will keep in an airtight container in the fridge for 4–5 days.

SERVES 1

It appears Tom Collins has many brothers - Joe (made with vodka), John (whiskey), Jose (tequila) and Pierre (Cognac). But the classic Tom, made with gin, is by far the most popular. For added wow factor - the blue floral gin turns purple with the addition of lemon juice.

Tom Collins Blue

55 g (¼ cup) caster (superfine) sugar

ice cubes

60 ml (¼ cup) Blue floral gin (page 23)

20 ml (¾ fl oz) lemon juice

chilled soda water (club soda), to top

lemon wheel, to garnish

maraschino cherry, to garnish

Make a simple syrup by combining the sugar and 60 ml (¼ cup) water in a small saucepan. Bring to the boil and stir until the sugar dissolves. Remove from the heat and leave to cool.

Place 4 or 5 ice cubes into a Collins glass. Add the gin, lemon juice and 15 ml (½ fl oz) of the simple syrup then use a long-stemmed spoon to mix well. Top with soda water and garnish with the lemon wheel and maraschino cherry.

SERVES 1

The Negroni is said to have been invented for a count in Florence, who wanted to add a little gin to his favourite refreshment. This white version was created more recently and the addition here of colourful nasturtium flowers adds a mild peppery note. With lots of colourful petals to pick from, it would be a bright addition to any dark evening.

Floral White Negroni

3 nasturtium flowers, plus 1 to garnish

1 large ice cube

40 ml (1¼ fl oz) dry gin

30 ml (1 fl oz) Lillet Blanc

30 ml (1 fl oz) Suze liqueur (or similar gentian-based liqueur)

Place the 3 flowers into a cocktail shaker and use a muddling tool to crush gently. Fill the shaker with ice and add the Lillet Blanc and Suze liqueur, then stir well.

Place the ice cube into a rocks glass and strain the cocktail over the ice. Serve garnished with a nasturtium.

SERVES 1

The elegant elderflower is known for its fragrant tones, and coupled with the earthiness of ginger the two combine for a modern twist on a Vodka martini. Elderflower liqueur is readily available in shops, and can be used to flavour all things edible.

Elderflower Martini

2.5 cm (1 in) piece ginger, thinly sliced

ice cubes

10 ml (¼ fl oz) elderflower liqueur

60 ml (¼ cup) vodka

10 ml (¼ fl oz) lemon juice

elderflower sprig, to garnish

Place the ginger into a cocktail shaker and use a muddling tool to gently crush.

Fill the shaker with ice and add the elderflower liqueur, vodka and lemon juice. Shake well for 30 seconds until well combined then strain into a chilled martini glass. Garnish with the elderflower sprig.

SERVES 1

No, you don't need to reach for the toolbox. This two-ingredient stirred-not-shaken cocktail in a highball hardly needs improvement, but the addition of a heavenly-scented citrus water, made from the crushed blossoms of the orange tree, amplifies its freshness.

Orange Blossom Screwdriver

ice cubes

45 ml (1½ fl oz) vodka

10 ml (¼ fl oz) orange blossom water

freshly squeezed orange juice, to top

orange twist, to garnish

Fill a highball glass with ice and add the vodka and orange blossom water. Top with orange juice and stir well to combine.

Garnish with the orange twist.

SERVES 1

The image of a purple haze of lavender on a sunny horizon conjures up the feeling of warm summer days. Lavender can be overpowering if used incorrectly, so tread lightly and taste as you go. This recipe is easily multiplied, perfect for impressing unannounced guests.

Lavender & Cucumber Smash

55 g (¼ cup) caster (superfine) sugar

2 teaspoons dried edible lavender flowers

1 short cucumber, peeled and roughly chopped

60 ml (2 fl oz) gin

crushed ice

fresh lavender sprigs, to garnish

Make a lavender syrup by combining the sugar, dried lavender and 60 ml (¼ cup) water in a small saucepan – add an extra teaspoon of lavender for a stronger taste. Bring to the boil and stir until the sugar dissolves. Remove from the heat and set aside for 30 minutes to infuse. Strain into a small bowl, discarding the solids.

Put the cucumber into a blender and blend to a fine mixture. Pass the mixture through a muslin-lined strainer into a small bowl, discarding the pulp.

Pour the gin, 20 ml (¾ fl oz) of the lavender syrup and 60 ml (2 fl oz) of the cucumber juice into a rocks glass then stir to combine. Top with crushed ice, and garnish with a lavender sprig.

The remaining lavender syrup will keep in an airtight container in the fridge for 4–5 days.

SERVES 1

When they finally have a woman play James Bond, you can picture her ordering a Rose martini, shaken, not stirred, as she surveys the room of a hotel bar, waiting for her mark. Any leftover rose syrup would be a nice addition to some sparkling water or even white wine.

Rose Martini

½ cup dried edible rose petals

115 g (½ cup) caster (superfine) sugar

ice cubes

50 ml (1¾ fl oz) gin

20 ml (¾ fl oz) dry vermouth

2–3 drops orange bitters

rose petal, to garnish

Make a rose petal syrup by combining the dried rose petals, sugar and 125 ml (½ cup) water in a small saucepan. Bring to the boil and stir until the sugar dissolves. Remove from the heat and leave to cool then refrigerate for 4 hours, or overnight for a stronger flavour. Strain into a small bowl, discarding the solids.

Fill a cocktail shaker with ice and add the gin, vermouth and 10 ml (¼ fl oz) of the rose syrup. Shake well for 30 seconds, then strain into a chilled martini glass. Top with a few drops of orange bitters and garnish with a rose petal.

The remaining rose petal syrup will keep in an airtight container in the fridge for 4–5 days.

SERVES 1

Pink, purple, violet, yellow, blue – the range of hues of the humble pansy are beautiful to behold, so pick your favourite here to really make it your own. The spritz renaissance is ongoing, the fizzy concoctions both easy to make and appealing to the masses.

Pansy Spritz

55 g (¼ cup) caster (superfine) sugar

5–6 pansies, plus 1 to garnish

ice cubes

30 ml (1 fl oz) gin

30 ml (1 fl oz) pear juice

chilled Champagne, to top

Make a pansy syrup by combining the sugar and 60 ml (¼ cup) water in a small saucepan. Bring to the boil and stir until the sugar dissolves. Place the pansies in a heatproof container and pour over the syrup. Mix, then cover and leave to infuse overnight in the fridge. Strain into a small bowl, discarding the solids.

Fill a cocktail shaker with ice and add the gin, pear juice and 10 ml (¼ fl oz) of the pansy syrup. Shake for 15 seconds then pour into a champagne flute. Top with chilled Champagne and garnish with a pansy.

The remaining pansy syrup will keep in an airtight container in the fridge for 4–5 days.

SERVES 1

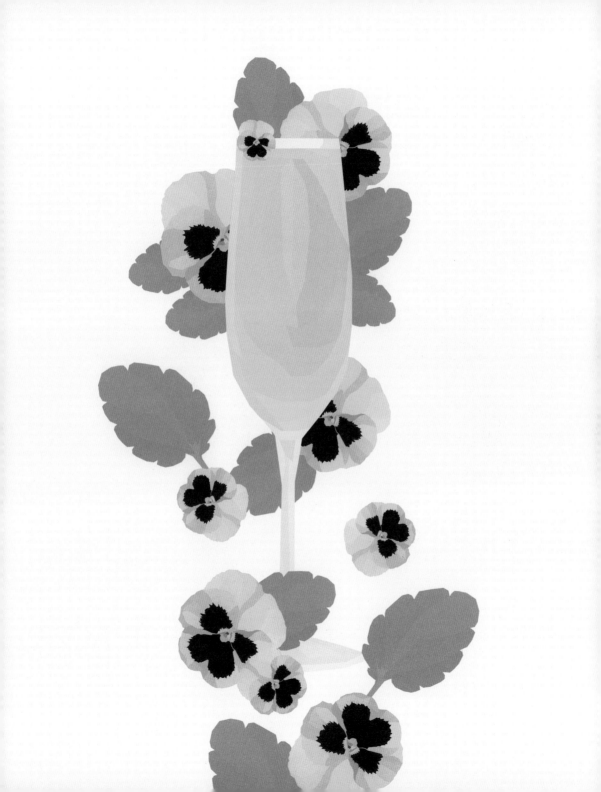

Silky and sour, with a hint of spring from the sweet-smelling jasmine, this cocktail is perfect sipped while reclining on a velvet chaise longue, as soft as the drink itself. Shaking the cocktail twice – once dry without ice and the second time with ice, leads to a thicker top layer.

Jasmine White Lady

1 jasmine teabag or
1 teaspoon jasmine tea leaves

50 ml (1¾ fl oz) dry gin

25 ml (¾ fl oz) orange liqueur

10 ml (¼ fl oz) lemon juice

10 ml (¼ fl oz) sugar syrup (page 48)

15 ml (½ fl oz) egg white or aquafaba

ice cubes

Place the teabag or tea leaves into 125 ml (½ cup) near-boiled water and leave to steep for 3–4 minutes. Remove the bag or strain the leaves from the tea and refrigerate until cold.

Place the gin, orange liqueur, lemon juice, sugar syrup, egg white or aquafaba and 10 ml (¼ fl oz) of the jasmine tea into a cocktail shaker and dry shake for 15 seconds. Add ice and shake for a further 15 seconds, then strain into a chilled cocktail glass.

SERVES 1

Here, the classic French 75, named for a military gun that had a bit of a kick, is given a floral makeover. The taste of lilac is characterised by sweet floral tones, with a hint of citrus, which is amplified in this recipe by pairing it with some fresh lemon juice.

Lilac French 75

55 g (¼ cup) caster (superfine) sugar

2 teaspoons edible lilac florets (purple flowers only)

ice cubes

30 ml (1 fl oz) gin

15 ml (½ fl oz) lemon juice

chilled Champagne, to top

lemon twist, to garnish

Make a lilac syrup by combining the sugar and 60 ml (¼ cup) water in a small saucepan. Bring to the boil and stir until the sugar dissolves. Add the lilacs, and simmer for 1–2 minutes. Remove from the heat and leave to cool, then transfer to an airtight container and leave to infuse for 4 hours or overnight in the fridge. Strain into a small bowl, discarding the solids.

Fill a cocktail shaker with ice and add the gin, lemon juice and 15 ml (½ fl oz) of the lilac syrup. Shake vigorously for 30 seconds, then strain into a champagne tulip. Top with Champagne and garnish with a lemon twist.

The remaining lilac syrup will keep in an airtight container in the fridge for 4–5 days.

SERVES 1

A cocktail for anyone who remembers a childhood spent sucking the nectar from the petals of the honeysuckle on warm summer days, found in hedgerows around the world. There are many species of the climbing plant, so be sure you know which species you are using.

Honeysuckle Sour

1 cup edible honeysuckle petals, green parts and leaves removed

170 g to 230 g (¾ to 1 cup) caster (superfine) sugar

ice cubes

40 ml (1¼ fl oz) tequila

20 ml (¾ fl oz) Chamomile gin (page 27)

20 ml (¾ fl oz) lime juice

50 ml (1¾ fl oz) pineapple juice

1 honeysuckle blossom, to garnish

Make a honeysuckle syrup by combining the honeysuckle and 250 ml (1 cup) near-boiled water in a heatproof container. Stir well then cover and leave to infuse in the fridge overnight. Strain the mixture through a muslin-lined strainer into a measuring jug and discard the solids. Add an equal measure of sugar then transfer to a small saucepan. Bring to the boil and stir until the sugar dissolves, then remove from the heat and allow to cool.

Fill a cocktail shaker with ice and add the tequila, gin, lime and pineapple juices and 20 ml (¾ fl oz) of the honeysuckle syrup. Shake well for 30 seconds, then strain into a tall glass filled with ice. Garnish with a honeysuckle blossom.

The remaining honeysuckle syrup will keep in an airtight container in the fridge for up to 1 week.

SERVES 1

Crème de violette, which lends this cocktail its hue, is made from wild violet blossoms, capturing the floral scent of the vibrant bloom. While it can be hard to find this liqueur and the cocktail can be made without it, it's worth seeking out for the full experience.

Aviation

ice cubes

60 ml (¼ cup) gin

15 ml (½ fl oz) lemon juice

10 ml (¼ fl oz) maraschino liqueur

15 ml (½ fl oz) crème de violette

edible violet, to garnish

lemon twist, to garnish

Fill a cocktail shaker with ice and add the gin, lemon juice, maraschino liqueur and crème de violette. Shake for 30 seconds until well combined, then strain into a chilled cocktail glass.

Garnish with an edible violet and a lemon twist.

SERVES 1

HERBACEOUS

Rosemary, native to the wild and rocky coast of the Mediterranean, has been valued for its medicinal properties since ancient times. When paired with gin and lemon juice, it does indeed have soothing properties ... though probably not in the same way. Pull out the drinks trolley and ease your weary bones with this value-added Rosemary gimlet.

Rosemary Gimlet

2 rosemary sprigs, plus an extra sprig to garnish

55 g (¼ cup) caster (superfine) sugar

ice cubes

60 ml (¼ cup) gin

30 ml (1 fl oz) lime juice

First make the rosemary syrup. Pick the leaves from two of the sprigs and roughly chop, then place into a small saucepan with the sugar and 60 ml (¼ cup) water. Bring to the boil and stir until the sugar dissolves. Remove from the heat and leave to infuse for 30 minutes. Pass the syrup through a muslin-lined strainer into a small bowl, discarding the solids.

Fill a cocktail shaker with ice and add the gin, lime juice and 15 ml (½ fl oz) of the rosemary syrup. Shake for 30 seconds until well combined, then strain into a chilled cocktail glass. Garnish with a sprig of rosemary.

The remaining rosemary syrup will keep in an airtight container in the fridge for 4–5 days.

SERVES 1

The cooling taste of mint on a hot day is a godsend to any parched individual - but let's add wine so that we can live like kings. The infused wine will enhance the flavour but for the lazy or time-poor among us, chilled white straight from the bottle will also work a treat.

Mint Spritz

ice cubes

150 ml (5 fl oz) Raspberry & mint wine, chilled (page 40)

2 mint leaves

3 raspberries, to garnish

chilled soda water (club soda), to top

Place 2 or 3 ice cubes in a wine glass, then add the wine, mint leaves and raspberries. Top with soda water and enjoy.

SERVES 1

A Bloody Mary can be accurately described as a meal in a glass – and for good reason, with some modern variations throwing in all but the kitchen sink. Here, blitzing the tomato juice with fresh parsley and coriander brings an earthy kick, perfect for a morning pick-me-up after, perhaps, one too many more sophisticated cocktails the night before.

Herby Bloody Mary

250 ml (1 cup) chilled tomato juice

large parsley sprig

large coriander (cilantro) sprig

ice cubes

45 ml (1½ fl oz) Garlic vodka (page 16)

15 ml (½ fl oz) lemon juice

celery salt, to taste

freshly ground black pepper, to taste

Worcestershire sauce, to taste

Tabasco sauce, to taste

1 celery stalk, to garnish

4 olives threaded on a cocktail stick, to garnish

Place the tomato juice, parsley and coriander in a blender, and blitz until the herbs are very fine and the mixture is well combined.

Fill a tall glass with ice cubes and add the vodka, lemon juice and tomato-herb mixture. Add celery salt, pepper, Worcestershire and Tabasco sauces to taste, stirring as you go.

Garnish with the olives and celery stalk.

SERVES 1

If travel isn't on the cards for you in the near future, it's still possible to close your eyes, sip this lemongrass-perfumed drink, and be transported to the bustling streets of Bangkok, or even farther afield to the blissful white beaches that hug the warm Andaman Sea.

Thai Lady

115 g (½ cup) caster (superfine) sugar

1 lemongrass stalk, white part only, chopped

ice cubes

40 ml (1¼ fl oz) gin

10 ml (¼ fl oz) triple sec

lemon wedge, to garnish

Make a lemongrass syrup by placing the sugar, lemongrass and 125 ml (½ cup) water into a small saucepan. Bring to the boil, stirring often, until the sugar dissolves, then leave to simmer for about 5 minutes. Remove from the heat, leave to cool and transfer to the fridge to infuse overnight. Strain into a small bowl, discarding the solids.

Fill a cocktail shaker with ice and add the gin, triple sec and 15 ml (½ fl oz) of the lemongrass syrup. Shake for 30 seconds until well combined, then strain into a glass. Serve with a lemon wedge.

The remaining lemongrass syrup will keep in an airtight container in the fridge for 4–5 days.

SERVES 1

Time may not be on our side, but you'll feel it slowing down as you sip this version of the classic Salty dog. Sometimes made with gin, but always with grapefruit juice, the addition of thyme adds a woody note to this 1920s-era tipple. Singing sea shanties is an optional extra.

Thyme Salty Dog

55 g (¼ cup) caster (superfine) sugar

3–4 thyme sprigs, plus an extra sprig to garnish

Himalayan pink salt, to garnish

lemon wedge

ice cubes, plus 1 large cube to garnish

60 ml (¼ cup) vodka

100 ml (3½ fl oz) pink grapefruit juice

lemon twist, to garnish

Make a thyme syrup by combining the sugar, thyme and 60 ml (¼ cup) water in a small saucepan. Bring to the boil and stir until the sugar dissolves. Remove from the heat and set aside for 30 minutes to infuse. Strain into a small bowl, discarding the solids.

Sprinkle some salt onto a small plate. Run the lemon wedge around the rim of an old-fashioned glass and dip the rim in the salt to coat. Place one large ice cube into the glass.

Fill a cocktail shaker with ice and add the vodka, pink grapefruit juice and 20 ml (¾ fl oz) of the thyme syrup. Shake for 10–15 seconds until well combined, then strain into the prepared glass. Garnish with a lemon twist.

The remaining thyme syrup will keep in an airtight container in the fridge for 4–5 days.

SERVES 1

The act of drinking coffee, sacred to many, can be traced back to the 15th century and shows no signs of going out of fashion. Here, the triple threat of coffee, chocolate and alcohol will leave you wide eyed and bushy tailed, but won't do much to help you sleep.

Espresso Martini

40 ml (1¼ fl oz) Chocolate vodka (page 19)

20 ml (¾ fl oz) espresso, chilled

20 ml (¾ fl oz) coffee liqueur

1 egg white or 30 ml (1 fl oz) aquafaba

10 ml (¼ fl oz) sugar syrup (page 48)

ice cubes

3 coffee beans, to garnish

Place all of the ingredients, except the ice and coffee beans, into a cocktail shaker and dry shake for 15 seconds. Add ice and shake for another 15 seconds.

Strain into a chilled martini glass and garnish with the coffee beans.

SERVES 1

Cinnamon, the dried bark of the cinnamon tree, is a warming spice, often used to add a little something extra to baked goods and hot drinks, perfect for any festive get-together. Paired with apple, this fire-in-a-glass will be as comforting as ... you guessed it: apple pie.

Apple Pie

½ teaspoon ground cinnamon

1 tablespoon caster (superfine) sugar

40 ml (1¼ fl oz) Cinnamon & apple whiskey (page 36)

20 ml (¾ fl oz) vodka

apple cider, to top

ice cubes

¼ red apple, thinly sliced, to garnish

Make a cinnamon-sugar garnish by mixing the cinnamon and sugar together on a small plate. Wet the rim of a tall glass, then press it into the cinnamon sugar to coat.

Fill the glass with ice. Pour in the whiskey and vodka, then use a stirrer to mix. Top with apple cider and garnish with the apple slices.

SERVES 1

Coriander, lime and jalapeño are a holy trinity of flavours, so to take it one step further to incorporate them in a glass is no big leap. This moreish, spicy drink goes well with tacos, quesadillas, or just with friends as the sun sets slowly in the background.

Coriander Margarita

55 g (¼ cup) caster (superfine) sugar

1 large coriander (cilantro) sprig, roughly chopped

salt

lime wedges

45 ml (1½ fl oz) tequila

30 ml (1 fl oz) Cointreau

30 ml (1 fl oz) lime juice

a few slices of jalapeño, thinly sliced (seeds optional), plus extra, to garnish

ice cubes

Make a coriander syrup by combining the sugar and 60 ml (¼ cup) water in a small saucepan. Bring to the boil and stir until the sugar dissolves. Remove from the heat, stir in the coriander and set aside for 30 minutes to infuse. Strain into a small bowl, discarding the coriander.

Place the salt on a plate. Run a lime wedge around the rim of a glass, then dip the rim in the salt.

Pour the tequila, Cointreau, lime juice and 25 ml (¾ fl oz) of the coriander syrup into a cocktail shaker. Add the sliced jalapeño and leave to infuse for 2 to 3 minutes. Fill the shaker with ice, shake well for 15 seconds then strain into the prepared glass. Garnish with a lime wedge and more jalapeño – as much as you fancy.

The remaining coriander syrup will keep in an airtight container in the fridge to 4–5 days.

SERVES 1

Prized for its flavour and perceived medicinal properties, ginger was a hot commodity along the ancient spice trade routes that spread to all corners of the globe. Often used as a palate cleanser, when paired with tequila it will wake up your taste buds in a flash.

Ginger Tequini

ice cubes

60 ml (¼ cup) Lemongrass & ginger tequila (page 35)

20 ml (¾ fl oz) dry vermouth

2 dashes Angostura bitters

lemon twist, to garnish

Fill a cocktail shaker with ice and add the tequila, vermouth and Angostura bitters. Shake well for 30 seconds until well combined then strain into a chilled martini glass.

Garnish with a lemon twist.

SERVES 1

Sage has been used since ancient times to treat all sorts of ailments. It was held in such regard that it was believed to impart a strength of memory to those who consumed it. Here, paired with bourbon, it may not have quite the same effect, but it will taste good.

Sage & Bourbon

5 sage leaves, plus 1 extra leaf to garnish

45 ml (1½ fl oz) bourbon

30 ml (1 fl oz) sweet vermouth

1 teaspoon honey

30 ml (1 fl oz) orange juice

ice cubes

Place the sage leaves, bourbon, sweet vermouth and honey in a cocktail shaker. Muddle the leaves with a muddling tool, then add the orange juice and a large handful of ice. Shake for 30 seconds until well combined, then strain into a rocks glass.

Garnish with a sage leaf.

SERVES 1

Matcha, made from finely powdered green tea leaves, is said to be packed with antioxidants, vitamins and other healing nutrients. It's even said to boost brain health – so it will balance out any brain cells you may kill with the sneaky addition of vodka. Not suitable for kids.

Matcha Lemonade

1 teaspoon matcha powder

40 ml (1¼ fl oz) vodka

25 ml (¾ fl oz) lemon juice

15 ml (½ fl oz) sugar syrup (page 48)

ice cubes

chilled soda water (club soda), to top

lemon slice, to garnish

Combine the matcha powder, vodka, lemon juice and sugar syrup in a cocktail shaker. Shake vigorously for 30 seconds – if the matcha has clumped, keep shaking until the mixture is smooth.

Fill a tall glass with ice and pour in the matcha mix. Top with soda water and serve with a straw or long-handled spoon to swirl, garnished with a lemon slice.

The remaining syrup will keep in an airtight container in the fridge for 4–5 days.

SERVES 1

All you will need to go with this refreshing tipple is a fan, a wide-brimmed hat and perhaps the sparkling Mediterranean in the distance. Pink peppercorns are surprisingly not pepper at all, but berries, which should give you something to mull over when imbibing this cocktail.

Pink Sipper

55 g (¼ cup) caster (superfine) sugar

2 teaspoons pink peppercorns, plus extra to garnish

ice cubes

50 ml (1¾ fl oz) Cucumber & mint gin (page 24)

chilled soda water (club soda), to top

mint sprig, to garnish

Make a peppercorn syrup by placing the sugar, pink peppercorns and 60 ml (¼ cup) water into a small saucepan – add an extra teaspoon of peppercorns if you like more of a kick. Bring to the boil and stir until the sugar dissolves. Remove from the heat and set aside for 30 minutes to infuse. Strain into a small bowl, discarding the solids.

Place a few ice cubes into a wine glass and add the gin and 15 ml (½ fl oz) of the peppercorn syrup. Top with soda water and use a stirrer to gently swirl, then garnish with a mint sprig and a few pink peppercorns.

The remaining peppercorn syrup will keep in an airtight container in the fridge for 4–5 days.

SERVES 1

A smash can be loosely used to describe an array of cocktails, but at its most basic it's liquor, syrup and something fresh. There are a multitude of variations, this one is fresh and green, and easy to master. The pungent aroma of fresh basil shouldn't be confined to the kitchen.

Lime Basil Smash

zest of 1 lime

1 tablespoon caster (superfine) sugar

lime wedge

ice cubes

small bunch basil, about 10 leaves, picked

60 ml (¼ cup) gin

20 ml (¾ fl oz) lime juice

15 ml (½ fl oz) sugar syrup (page 48)

basil sprig, to garnish

Make a lime-sugar garnish by mixing the lime zest and sugar together on a small plate. Run the wedge of lime around the rim of a rocks glass, then press the wet rim into the lime sugar. Fill the glass with ice.

Place the basil into a cocktail shaker and muddle gently. Add the gin, lime juice and sugar syrup and fill with ice cubes, then shake for 30 seconds or until well combined. Strain into the prepared glass and garnish with fresh basil.

SERVES 1

FRUITY

The combination of rum, lime and a little something sweet was no doubt a staple in Cuba before 1896, but it wasn't until then that it was christened a Daquiri by a visiting American engineer, or so the story goes. The OG Daquiri is simple and elegant, and the addition of the black-flecked flesh of the dragon fruit makes for an interesting-looking cocktail.

Dragon Daquiri

1 dragon fruit, with 1 wedge saved to garnish

ice cubes

20 ml (¾ fl oz) lime juice

60 ml (¼ cup) Pineapple rum (page 31)

5 ml (¼ fl oz) sugar syrup (page 48)

Peel the dragon fruit, cut into chunks and puree in a mini blender, adding a splash of water if needed to loosen it up.

Fill a cocktail shaker with ice and add the lime juice, rum, sugar syrup and 20 ml (¾ fl oz) of the dragon fruit puree. Shake for 30 seconds until well combined, then use a large-holed strainer to strain into a cocktail glass. Garnish with a wedge of dragon fruit.

The remaining puree keep in an airtight container in the fridge for 3 days.

SERVES 1

A bit younger than the other cocktails (only created in the mid-1980s), the Bramble gets its blackberry flavour from crème de mûre, layered here with the delicate berry itself. A hint of rosemary adds an earthy tone to a modern classic, and you can forage the berries yourself.

Bramble

1 rosemary sprig

6 blackberries

crushed ice

50 ml (1¾ fl oz) gin

20 ml (¾ fl oz) lemon juice

20 ml (¾ fl oz) rosemary syrup (page 72)

20 ml (¾ fl oz) crème de mûre

Remove the needles from the bottom two-thirds of the rosemary sprig, then thread 3 blackberries onto the stem. Fill a tumbler with crushed ice.

Place the gin, lemon juice, rosemary syrup and remaining 3 blackberries into a cocktail shaker, then use a muddling tool to firmly crush the berries. Shake for 15 seconds until well combined, then strain into the prepared tumbler. Drizzle the crème de mûre over the ice, so that it trickles down, and garnish with the prepared rosemary sprig.

SERVES 1

If you think that tequila is only for licking, drinking and shooting, then think again. This rosy-hued Mexican cocktail is a favourite the world over. Paloma is the Spanish word for dove and, like doves, this cocktail can be effectively released at festive occasions.

Paloma

2 pink grapefruit wedges

coarse sea salt

ice cubes

45 ml (1½ fl oz) tequila

15 ml (½ fl oz) agave syrup

15 ml (½ fl oz) lime juice

juice from ½ pink grapefruit

chilled soda water (club soda), to top

Run one of the grapefruit wedges around the rim of a tall glass, dip the rim into the salt to coat, then fill the glass with ice.

Pour the tequila, agave syrup, lime and pink grapefruit juices into the glass, then top with soda water and stir well.

SERVES 1

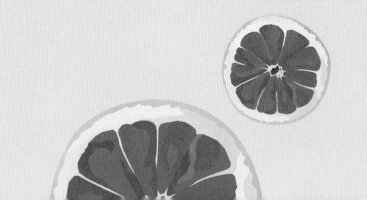

If you like Lychee coladas ... then you've come to the right place. While it can't guarantee you'll get caught in the rain, this smooth concoction will make you a bit happier if you happen to have wet feet, and it even comes with an umbrella. Good with some 80s tunes.

Lychee Colada

3 lychees, peeled and pitted

60 ml (¼ cup) white rum

60 ml (¼ cup) coconut cream

60 ml (¼ cup) coconut water

ice cubes

pineapple wedge and a maraschino cherry, threaded onto a paper umbrella

Place the lychees, rum, coconut cream and water and a handful of ice into a blender and blitz until smooth.

Serve in a tall glass garnished with the prepared paper umbrella.

SERVES 1

Something doesn't hang around for a couple of hundred years without attracting some imitations. This take on the classic Old fashioned is fruity, while still keeping the four core ingredients - sugar, bitters, liquor and water. Feel free to use any whiskey of your choice.

Peachy Old Fashioned

1 sugar cube

2 dashes Angostura bitters

3 peach slices, plus 1 extra slice to garnish

chilled soda water (club soda)

ice cubes

60 ml (¼ cup) bourbon

Place the sugar cube, Angostura bitters, peach slices and a splash of soda water in a rocks glass. Use a muddling tool to break down the sugar and crush the peach slices. Rotate the glass on its side, so that the mixture coats the inside of the glass. Add ice then pour over the bourbon.

Garnish with a peach slice.

SERVES 1

With a perfect little orb of rum-soaked cherry in each glass, there really is one for everybody in the audience. And, when a party calls for something a little festive, bubbles are always the answer, so pop a cork or two and let the good times roll.

Moonshine Cherry Fizz

120 ml (4 fl oz) Cherry rum plus 8 moonshine cherries (page 28)

1 bottle sparkling white wine

Divide the cherry rum among eight champagne flutes. Top with chilled sparkling wine and garnish each drink with a moonshine cherry.

SERVES 8

Created in the 1850s in New Orleans, the Brandy crusta is identifiable by its sugar-crusted rim and long, thick lemon peel garnish, called a horse's neck. It's a classic for a reason – citrus flavours mingle with cherry and Cognac, for a sweet, boozy sensation.

Brandy Crusta

peel of half a lemon, plus a wedge

granulated sugar

ice cubes

50 ml (1¾ fl oz) Cognac

20 ml (¾ fl oz) Cointreau

15 ml (½ fl oz) lemon juice

5 ml (¼ fl oz) maraschino liqueur

Angostura bitters, to garnish

Run the lemon wedge around the rim of a stemmed cocktail glass then dip into the sugar to coat. Place the lemon peel inside the glass.

Fill a cocktail shaker with ice and add the Cognac, Cointreau, lemon juice and maraschino liqueur. Shake for 30 seconds until well combined then strain into the prepared glass.

Garnish with 2 or 3 drops of Angostura bitters.

SERVES 1

The devil is in the detail, and in this case the detail is a spicy chilli-infused tequila. You can also use straight tequila and the drink will still be a delicious treat. Shake up this mix of makrut lime, ginger and blackcurrant with plenty of ice to cool down on a hot, hot day.

Makrut El Diablo

55 g (¼ cup) caster (superfine) sugar

3 makrut lime leaves, sliced, plus 1 more to garnish

ice cubes

60 ml (¼ cup) Habanero & lime tequila (page 32)

10 ml (¼ fl oz) crème de cassis

15 ml (½ fl oz) lime juice

chilled ginger beer, to top

Make a makrut lime syrup by combining the sugar, sliced makrut lime leaves and 60 ml (¼ cup) water in a small saucepan. Bring to the boil and stir until the sugar dissolves. Remove from the heat and set aside for 2 –3 hours to infuse. Strain into a small bowl, discarding the leaves.

Fill a tall glass with ice.

Fill a cocktail shaker with ice and add the tequila, crème de cassis, lime juice and 10 ml (¼ fl oz) of the makrut lime syrup. Shake for 30 seconds until well combined, then strain into the prepared glass. Top with the ginger beer and garnish with a makrut lime leaf.

The remaining makrut lime syrup will keep in an airtight container in the fridge for up to 5 days.

SERVES 1

While the battle between Chile and Peru for who created pisco may be ongoing, there should be no fighting when consuming this sour classic with friends. A touch of apple gives this already fresh drink an extra hit. Omit the bitters if you prefer the Chilean version.

Pisco Apple Sour

60 ml (2 fl oz) pisco

10 ml (¼ fl oz) lime juice

30 ml (1 fl oz) fresh apple juice

1 teaspoon honey

1 egg white or 30 ml (1 fl oz) aquafaba

ice cubes

Angostura bitters, to garnish (optional)

Place the pisco, lime juice, apple juice, honey and egg white or aquafaba into a cocktail shaker and dry shake for 15 seconds. Add ice and shake for another 15 seconds. Strain into a glass and garnish with 3 drops of Angostura bitters, if desired.

SERVES 1

Sparkle, sparkle, everywhere and plenty of bubbles to drink. This recipe is easily multiplied to satisfy you and all of your booze-hound friends. With a little time you can infuse your own raspberry vodka, swapping the strawberry and basil for raspberries, as seen on page 12.

French Sparkle

1 mango, peeled and flesh diced

ice cubes

45 ml (1½ fl oz) raspberry-flavoured vodka

chilled sparkling white wine, to top

2 frozen raspberries

Make mango juice by placing the mango and 125 ml (½ cup) water into a blender, and blitz until smooth. Check and adjust consistency if needed by adding more water. Pass the juice through a fine-mesh sieve into a small bowl.

Fill a cocktail shaker with ice and add the vodka, 30 ml (1 fl oz) of the mango juice, and a dash of sparkling wine. Use a stirrer to mix well then strain into a chilled martini glass and garnish with the frozen raspberries.

The remaining mango juice will keep in an airtight container in the fridge for 3 days.

SERVES 1

The traditional mix of muddled mint, lime, rum and soda is hard to beat, but we might as well try. The addition of the fairest fruit, the strawberry, lends this version a plummy pink hue. It is sure to impress your friends as they see you putting a little more effort than usual into your regular 6 o'clock gathering at the drinks trolley.

Strawberry Mojito

4 strawberries

8 mint leaves

20 ml (¾ fl oz) lime juice

1 teaspoon granulated sugar

60 ml (¼ cup) white rum

ice cubes

chilled soda water (club soda), to top

Place the strawberries, mint, lime juice and sugar in a tall glass and muddle well. Add a few ice cubes to the glass and then the rum. Top with soda water and stir well.

Serve with a paper straw, if desired.

SERVES 1

Sounding more like an upmarket speakeasy than a drink, the clover club has been around since before Prohibition, which brought the rise in the popularity of the cocktail. Here, the classic is given a twist with fresh raspberries instead of grenadine – we'll happily join this club.

Clover Club

55 g (¼ cup) caster (superfine) sugar

4 raspberries, plus 3 raspberries on a cocktail stick, to garnish

60 ml (¼ cup) raspberry gin

20 ml (¾ fl oz) lemon juice

1 egg white or 30 ml (1 fl oz) aquafaba

ice cubes

Make a raspberry syrup by combining the sugar and 60 ml (¼ cup) water in a small saucepan. Bring to the boil and stir until the sugar dissolves. Remove from the heat and add the 4 raspberries, using a fork to crush them. Set aside to cool, then push the mixture through a fine-mesh sieve into a small bowl, discarding the solids.

Place the gin, lemon juice, egg white or aquafaba, and 20 ml (¾ fl oz) of the raspberry syrup into a cocktail shaker and dry shake for 15 seconds. Add ice and shake for another 15 seconds. Strain into a chilled coupe and garnish with the prepared cocktail stick.

The remaining raspberry syrup will keep in an airtight container in the fridge for up to 5 days.

SERVES 1

One of the most well known cocktails, the Tequila sunrise has taken on a gimmicky persona over the past few decades, rather unfairly. With a hint of chilli from infused tequila, you'll feel the burn from this glass of sunshine, as if the sun itself is coming up to bathe you in its glow.

Tequila Hot Sunrise

125 ml (½ cup) orange juice

60 ml (¼ cup) Habanero & lime tequila (page 32)

ice cubes

20 ml (¾ fl oz) grenadine syrup

1 maraschino cherry, to garnish

1 orange slice, to garnish

Pour the orange juice and tequila into a tall glass and stir well until combined, then add ice. Use the back of a spoon to pour the grenadine down the inside side of the glass, allowing it to settle to the bottom.

Garnish with the maraschino cherry and orange slice.

SERVES 1

'Why is it called a mule?' is a question often asked, probably by not that many people. Well, mule comes from buck, supposedly, which came from horse's neck. Wherever it came from, this ruby-red version of a bar room staple sure delivers on its kick. Bottoms up.

Pomegranate Moscow Mule

ice cubes

60 ml (¼ cup) vodka

60 ml (¼ cup) pomegranate juice

15 ml (½ fl oz) lime juice

chilled ginger beer, to top

1 tablespoon pomegranate seeds

Fill a rocks glass with ice.

Fill a cocktail shaker with ice and add the vodka, pomegranate and lime juices. Shake for 30 seconds until well combined. Strain into the prepared glass then top with ginger beer and sprinkle over the pomegranate seeds.

SERVES 1

PUNCHES

Punches are perfect for parties - the very essence of a punch is a drink to be shared. This one is ideal for when you are after something a little lighter and less alcoholic, so that your all-day gathering doesn't become an all-night one, complete with rowdy guests.

All Day Passion Punch

5 passionfruit

a few mint sprigs

ice cubes

1 bottle chilled Prosecco

80 ml (⅓ cup) vodka

1 litre (4 cups) chilled soda water (club soda)

500 ml (2 cups) pineapple juice

Slice 1 of the passionfruit into wedges. Remove the pulp from the remaining 4 passionfruit and place into a large pitcher along with the mint sprigs. Muddle slightly then add ice, then add the Prosecco, vodka, soda water and pineapple juice. Add the passion fruit wedges and stir gently to combine.

SERVES 10-12

There's a good reason why Mary Poppins' special medicine was the flavour of rum punch – it's soothing, warming, and perfect for when you've gotten your feet wet. This warm party punch is practically perfect in every way, and especially great for sipping by an open fire.

Cloudy Pear Rum Punch

handful crystallised ginger, to serve

2 limes, cut into wedges

1.5 litres (6 cups) cloudy pear juice

125 ml (½ cup) water

2 cinnamon sticks

1 tablespoon brown sugar

3 cm (1¼ in) piece ginger, peeled and thinly sliced

500 ml (2 cups) golden rum

1 pear, thinly sliced

Thread some cocktail sticks each with a chunk of crystallised ginger and a wedge of lime – enough for your guests – and set aside.

Pour the pear juice and water into a saucepan and add the cinnamon sticks, sugar and fresh ginger. Bring to the boil, then reduce the heat and simmer for 4–5 minutes, stirring occasionally. Remove from the heat then stir in the rum and add the pear slices.

Serve in heatproof glasses, garnished with the cocktail sticks – those who want a twist can squeeze the lime if they wish.

SERVES 8-10

The scent and subtle taste of rose petals adds a dreamy, perfumed flavour to this punch, perfect for your next lazy summer afternoon get-together. Best served to your closest friends in a sprawling rose garden, so that you can literally smell the roses.

Wild Rose Punch

1 bottle chilled sparkling rose wine

60 ml (¼ cup) gin

500 ml (2 cups) chilled soda water (club soda)

80 ml (⅓ cup) rose petal syrup (page 59)

ice cubes

handful fresh rose petals, washed, or dried rose petals to garnish

In a pitcher, combine the sparkling rose, gin, soda water and rose petal syrup. Add ice cubes and stir well to combine.

Garnish with fresh or dried rose petals.

SERVES 6-8

The frozen Margarita definitely falls on the fun side of the punch scale. Super cooling and made in just a few minutes with the help of your blender, this variation of the Margarita (there are a few!) is sure to please. Frozen blueberries are preferred but not essential.

Frozen Blueberry & Rosemary Margaritas

6 small rosemary sprigs

185 ml (¾ cup) orange liqueur

250 ml (1 cup) tequila blanco

60 ml (¼ cup) lime juice

60 ml (¼ cup) rosemary syrup (page 72)

3 cups frozen blueberries

2 cups ice cubes

Remove the leaves from the bottom half of each rosemary sprig. Set aside.

Place the remaining ingredients in a blender, and blitz to a fine mixture. Divide between six margarita glasses and garnish each glass with a prepared rosemary sprig.

SERVES 6

If you can't make it to Wimbledon this year to watch the tennis, the solution is simple: invite all your friends around on a hot day, give everyone a glass or two of Pimm's punch, then take turns swearing at a make-believe umpire. Game, set and a rather boozy match.

Pimm's Punch

4 blood oranges

2 lemons

1 tablespoon caster (superfine) sugar

small bunch mint, leaves picked

400 ml (13½ fl oz) Pimm's No. 1

1 short cucumber, thinly sliced

200 g (7 oz) strawberries, hulled and quartered

1 bottle chilled Champagne

ice cubes

Juice 3 of the oranges and 1 lemon. In a punch bowl or large jug, combine the juices, sugar and half the mint leaves. Muddle gently, then add the Pimm's No. 1. Stir well, until the sugar has dissolved.

Slice the remaining orange and lemon into thin rounds. Add the slices, along with the cucumber, strawberries and plenty of ice to the punch. Add the Champagne slowly and gently stir.

Use a ladle to serve, ensuring each of your guests gets some ice and fruit, as well as punch.

SERVES 8-10

Strawberries and basil have a proven track record as a match made in heaven, and vodka has a knack of making everything taste better. Freeze is just a grown-up way to say slushie, but a Basil slushie would sound a bit too juvenile for this light and fun summer cooler.

Basil Freeze

300 g (10½ oz) frozen strawberries

200 ml (7 fl oz) Strawberry & basil vodka (page 12)

1 tablespoon honey

1 cup ice cubes

Place all the ingredients in a blender, and blitz to a fine puree. Pour into short glasses, and garnish with a basil leaf.

SERVES 4

Who needs ice when you can make it from fruit? You can boast to your guests that you're providing food and drink in one handy glass, saving on the washing up. You may even convince them (with a wink) that they're getting one of their five-a-day.

Berry Good Punch

155 g (1 cup) blueberries

125 g (1 cup) raspberries

130 g (1 cup) blackberries

375 ml (1½ cups) vodka

125 ml (½ cup) peach liqueur

360 g (2 cups) frozen black or purple grapes

1.5 litres (6 cups) chilled soda water (club soda)

Place a third of the berries into a blender along with 60 ml (¼ cup) water and blend to a puree. Pass the puree through a fine-mesh sieve, discarding the seeds.

Place the puree into a large jug or punch bowl and add the vodka, peach liqueur, frozen grapes and remaining berries. Stir well to combine and top with the soda water.

Stir well before serving, using a ladle to give everyone some fruit in their drink.

SERVES 10-12

Chamomile has been used for thousands of years to soothe and proclaims to have all kinds of health benefits. You can rattle that off when divvying up this cocktail between five of your closest friends, in any situation where iced tea or lemonade just won't do.

Chamomile Gin Cooler

250 ml (1 cup) Chamomile gin (page 27)

80 ml (⅓ cup) pear liqueur

60 ml (¼ cup) sugar syrup (page 48)

60 ml (¼ cup) lemon juice

1 bottle chilled sparkling wine

ice cubes

1 pear, thinly sliced, to garnish

Pour the gin, pear liqueur, sugar syrup and lemon juice into a jug, and stir to combine. Divide between six glasses and top each with sparkling wine. Add an ice cube and garnish with a pear slice.

SERVES 6

You can understand why the translation of 'sangria' from Spanish to English means bleeding – given the red wine it's traditionally made from. Sangria blanco, a more recent version, using white wine instead of red, is less traditional but still a great reason for a party.

Sparkling Melon Sangria

1 small honeydew melon

1 small cantaloupe (rockmelon)

½ small seedless watermelon

1 bottle Moscato wine

1 bottle chilled sparkling white wine

250 ml (1 cup) dry ginger ale

small bunch mint, leaves picked

Start this recipe the day before serving. Remove and discard the seeds from the honeydew melon and cantaloupe. Use a melon baller to ball all three melons – you should have about 2 cups of each fruit. Place the balls in a pitcher and add the Moscato, then gently stir. Cover and refrigerate overnight.

When ready to serve, add the sparkling wine, ginger ale and mint and stir gently to combine. To serve, use a ladle to give everyone some fruit in their drink.

SERVES 6-8

The bright star of parties in the colder months, mulled wine has long been used to revive and warm guests as they step in from the cold, perhaps brushing a touch of snow from their lapels. As an added bonus, the smells of orange, cinnamon and star anise will fill your home.

Mulled Wine

3 oranges

6 cloves, plus more for garnish

1.5 litres (6 cups) red wine

60 ml (¼ cup) brandy

115 g (½ cup) brown sugar

3 cinnamon sticks

4 star anise

Cut one orange into slices then half-moon slices, then pierce each wedge with 2 cloves to garnish and set aside.

Juice the two remaining oranges. Place the juice, wine, brandy, sugar, cinnamon sticks, 6 cloves and star anise into a saucepan. Taking great care (see page 9), heat over a medium heat until steaming, then reduce the heat to low and cook for a further 5 minutes. The wine will become more spiced the longer you cook it, so taste and remove from the heat once it's reached your desired level of spice.

Serve in heatproof mugs or cups, with a clove-studded orange slice to garnish.

SERVES 10

Index

Published in 2022 by Smith Street Books
Naarm | Melbourne | Australia
smithstreetbooks.com

ISBN: 978-1-922417-33-6

Publisher: Paul McNally
Editor and text: Aisling Coughlan
Illustrations: Annabelle Lambie
Designer: Michelle Mackintosh
Typesetter: Heather Menzies
Proofreader: Pamela Dunne
Indexer: Helena Holmgren

Printed & bound in China by C&C Offset Printing Co., Ltd.

Book 222
10 9 8 7 6 5 4